D1444319

WITHDRAWN

Canadian Trees

Canadian Trees

Copyright © 1994 by Colleayn O. Mastin

Canadian Cataloguing in Publication Data

Mastin, Colleayn, O. (Colleayn Olive)
    Canadian Trees

Nature Canada Series; 3

        ISBN 1-895910-02-1 (bound). - ISBN
        1-89510-05-6 (pbk.)
        1. Trees—Canada—Juvenile literature.
        I. Sovak, Jan, 1953- II. Title.   III. Series.
        QK201..M388 1994 j.582.160971 C93-091871-1

PUBLISHED BY~

GRASSHOPPER BOOKS
106 - WADDINGTON DRIVE
KAMLOOPS, BRITISH COLUMBIA
CANADA V2E 1M2

This book is dedicated to January, Tiffany, Lindsay, Jody and Adrianne-Monique.

A portion of the sales
of this book will be
donated to the
Canadian Nature Federation

Acknowledgement

The author wishes to thank the following individuals for their contributions to this book ~ Francoise Sveistrup, Dr. Hubert Bunce, Dean Purych, Dan Holden, Barry Kenoras, Ken Uyeda, Wendy Nankivell, Kathryn Burkell, Dennis Johnson

DESIGN & PRODUCTION BY ~ BLACKBIRD DESIGN, CALGARY, ALBERTA
PRINTED IN CANADA BY ~ FRIESEN PRINTERS LTD., ALTONA, MANITOBA

Aspen

In every part of Canada,
These white-trunked trees are found
For "trembling" aspen feel at home
In many types of ground.

We call them "trembling" aspen
Because even a gentle breeze,
Will start their round leaves quiveri
In groves of aspen trees.

If you ever get lost in the woods, an aspen tree
uld help by letting
u know in what
ection you are
ing. The chalky white material that is found on
bark is always thickest on the south side of the
e.

Aspen is used to make paper, toilet tissue,
tches, plywood, boxes and snowboards. This
e is a tasty food for the beaver. Native people
ce ate the inner bark, raw or roasted. They also
led it the "noisy leaf tree" because of the sound
nakes when the wind blows.

Fir

Firs are graceful, tall, strong tree
With narrow pointed crowns;
These trees make jobs for people
In dozens of lumbering towns.

The largest tree that gro
in Canada is the Douglas

You can tell the differe
between fir and spruce need
by rolling them between yo
finger and thumb. Spruce need
will roll, while fir needles are

e tallest firs seem to touch the sky,

they sway in a wind or a breeze;

ch smaller firs we set on stands

d call them Christmas trees.

d will not roll.

hen grows on the branches of the Douglas fir.

is is a very important food for the caribou in the forest.

hen the wind blows the lichen falls off the branches

d the caribou eat them for winter food.

r is used for building houses because the

od is very strong.

Cedar

Some Native Indian people used to make their canoes out of birch bark, though the West Coast Indians still carve magnificent canoes and totem pole from the mighty cedar. Years ago, they used the tree's stringy bark to weave cloth for clothing and blankets.

Longhouses, where the people of some communit lived, were also made from cedar logs.

Many forest birds use this tree for their nests. The spotted owl builds its nest in holes in the trunk and th majestic bald eagle builds its nest on the very top.

Cedar wood does not rot quickly, so it is very good for fence posts, cedar shakes, roofs and for the sidin of houses.

A yellow cedar seed once planted, can ta up to two thousand years to become a giant tree. A red cedar takes abo one thousand years to become a gigantic tre

The cedar tree has stringy bark,
Its dark green leaves lie flat;
This scented wood makes trunks and chests,
To store your coat and hat.

And from its soft and straight-grained wood,
We make shingles, shakes and siding,
And all those lines of cedar fence
You can see when you go riding.

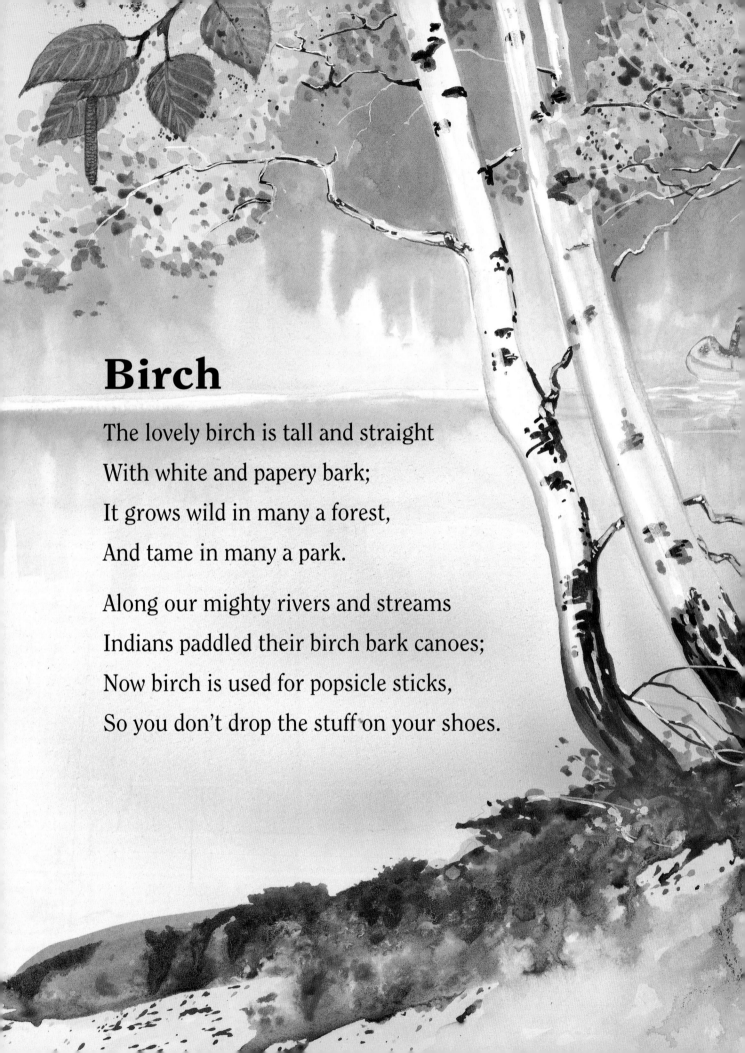

Birch

The lovely birch is tall and straight
With white and papery bark;
It grows wild in many a forest,
And tame in many a park.

Along our mighty rivers and streams
Indians paddled their birch bark canoes;
Now birch is used for popsicle sticks,
So you don't drop the stuff on your shoes.

The wood from birch trees is used to make wonderful things like toys, school desks, bookcases, paper, boxes and skate-boards. When you go skating down the street, remember, that's a tree beneath your feet. Native people used this tree to make baskets and canoes.

The birch tree normally grows in open areas. If you peel the bark from a dead birch, it can be used as a good starter for campfires. The birch is the provincial tree of Saskatchewan.

Hemlock

You can tell this tree's a hemlock
By the top branch of its crown,
For its slender, whip-like "leader"
Gracefully droops down.

Native Indians used hemlock bark
To make bread they loved to munch;
And from hemlock pulp comes cellophane
That we use to wrap our lunch.

The tiny seeds that fall from the cones of the hemlock have wings that can carry them through the air to find a spot where they can sprout and grow. These seeds are food for birds and mice, while rabbits and beavers eat the tender little seedlings. Deer will eat the leaves and twigs from older trees.

Because the roots of hemlock trees do not grow deep into the ground, sometimes snow and wind will topple them. Those that do survive, can live for four or five hundred years.

Hemlock is a very important tree in the lumber industry. It is used to build houses, and to make cardboard boxes, telephone poles, broom handles, and paper.

Sitka spruce is the tallest, though not the largest, of our native trees. In the early days of flying, many airplanes were made out of Sitka spruce.

Many centuries ago, when the explorer Jacques Cartier and his men were suffering from the disease called scurvy, the Indians gave them tea made from spruce needles. This helped them to get well.

Native people of the west coast used the roots and branches of the spruce trees to weave hats and to make baskets. The gum from the tree is now used to make candy, chewing gum, and medicine.

Spruce is a very important tree for the lumber industry. It is used for building houses, and for making plywood, crates, cabinets, and paper.

pruce

...is very tall and straight trunked tree,
...an evergreen called the spruce;
...grows all over Canada
...d of it we make great use.

...s especially good for paper,
... next time you have a cold,
...d reach for a piece of tissue,
...at's part of a spruce you hold.

Forests

Imagine a world without forests;
How awful it would be,
To travel across our country
And never see a tree.

Our forests give us many things,
Wild birds and some bears live there,
Without forests, we would not have,
That wonderful stuff called air.

Forests are called "The Lungs of the Earth". The leaves of trees give off the oxygen which is important to all creatures who breathe. This is one of the main reasons we must see that the forests of the world are maintained.

Trees provide shade for animals and humans. They also act as windbreaks to shelter crops and homes, hold the soil in place with their roots, and provide beauty for all to see.

The forest is home for wild animals and birds. People, such as birdwatchers, hikers, swimmers, painters, photographers, berry pickers, and fishermen all share the forest with the animals. The forest also provides the raw materials for products such as paper, lumber, and medicines.

Tamarack

The northern swamps of Canada
Are home to the tamarack;
From its wood we make the ties
That carry a railroad track.

Since the tamarack's a conifer,
It should stay green all year,
But its needles turn yellow in fal
And get scattered far and near.

The tamarack tree is special because it is a cone-bearing evergreen and should keep its needles all year but it does not.

It drops its needles in the fall like the leaves of a deciduous tree. Then, in the spring, the tamarack needles grow back again, just the same as the leaves that grow back on deciduous trees.

Tamarack is used to make pulp for books, newspapers, railway ties, and for building construction lumber. Tannin, a substance used for tanning leather, is taken from the bark of the tamarack.

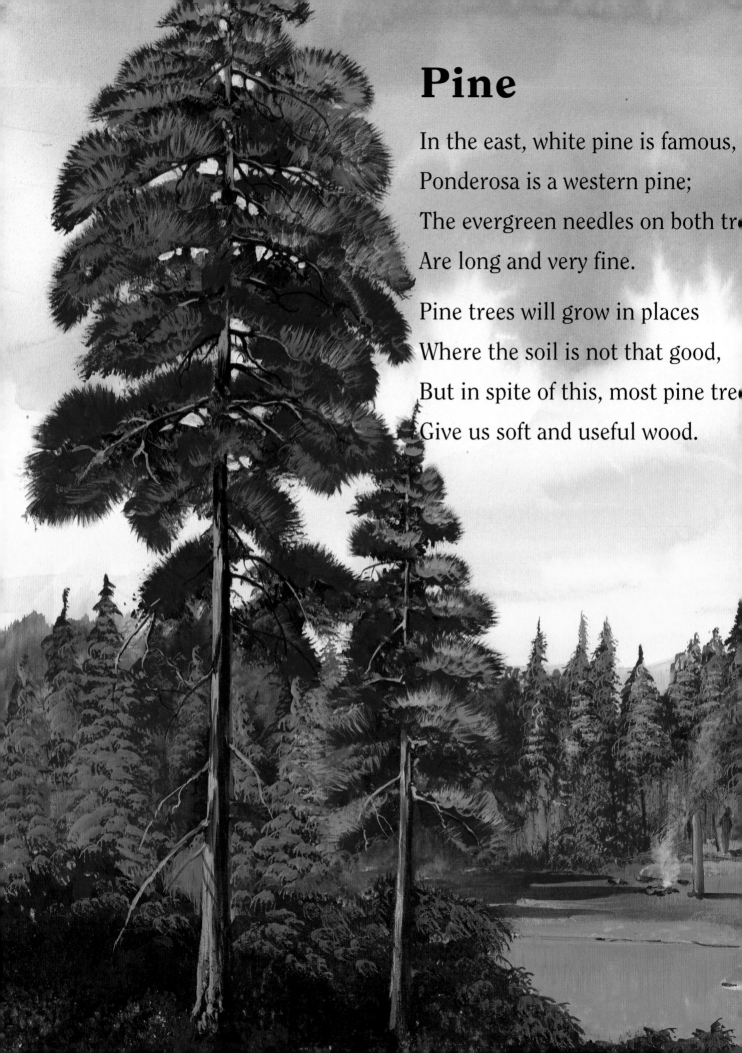

Pine

In the east, white pine is famous,
Ponderosa is a western pine;
The evergreen needles on both tr[ees]
Are long and very fine.

Pine trees will grow in places
Where the soil is not that good,
But in spite of this, most pine tre[es]
Give us soft and useful wood.

The Ponderosa pine is sometimes called the "Jig-Saw Tree". The bark of older trees flakes off into chunks that look like the pieces of a jig-saw puzzle.

There are over thirty kinds of pines growing in Canada. One pine tree is named the lodgepole pine. This tree grows tall, straight, and slim. Because of this, native people used this tree for building tepees and lodges. They also used the inner bark, which they boiled and mashed to make bread. The sweet orange sap is also good to eat.

If you look around your house, you will probably see pine wood that has been used to make doors, window frames, wooden matches, boxes, crates, and the cabinets in your kitchen. The early settlers in Canada used pine for making furniture. The white pine is the official tree of Ontario.

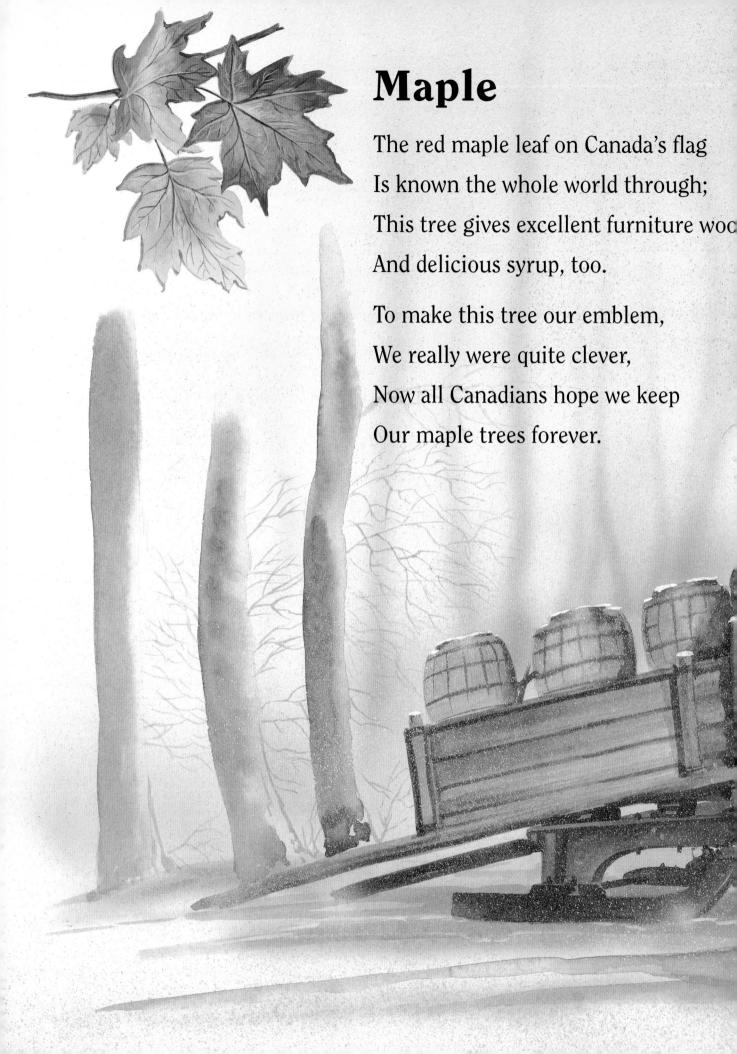

Maple

The red maple leaf on Canada's flag
Is known the whole world through;
This tree gives excellent furniture woo[d]
And delicious syrup, too.

To make this tree our emblem,
We really were quite clever,
Now all Canadians hope we keep
Our maple trees forever.

Not all maple trees produce the sap that can be turned into maple syrup or maple sugar. The best sugar maples grow in eastern Canada. It takes about thirty litres of maple sap to make one litre of this wonderful, sweet-tasting syrup for our pancakes.

This tree is very important for wildlife. Birds build their nests in these beautiful trees and also feed on the seeds. Deer eat the young twigs and buds. Porcupine eat the bark, but if they strip it totally around the trunk, they can kill this handsome tree. The maple leaf was chosen for the Canadian flag in 1965.

Fruit Trees

All of our trees are useful
For the good things that they bring,
But fruit trees are quite special,
For they blossom in the spring.

Some bear sweet fruit in autumn,
That we and the birds can share;
So let's give thanks for the apple and plum,
The cherry, the peach and the pear.

The fruit trees that we have in the orchards were brought here by the first settlers that came to homestead in Canada.

Just as they brought cows, sheep, goats, pigs and other animals that were not native to Canada, pioneers also brought grafts of the fruit trees from their old country homes so that they could grow them in orchards here. They blossom in the spring and bear fruit in the summer and fall.

Some animals, such as deer, horses, cows and birds, enjoy eating the fruits that grow in the orchard. The leaves and bark of some fruit trees can be used to make medicine.

Oak

The oak is called the "King of Trees;
Its growth is long and slow;
You'd wonder how such mighty oa
From tiny acorns grow.

There are many types of oak trees
To name them might get boring,
But one thing should be noted—
These trees make great oak floorin

Oak is also used to make chairs, tables, beds, desks, and railings for buildings and boats.

There is an old legend that says when the last oak tree dies on Oak Island, (located off the coast of Nova Scotia), a treasure buried there, under an oak tree by pirates, will, at last, be found.

Acorns from the mighty oak are an important food for deer, bears, squirrels and other rodents. Many birds, including the woodpecker, jay, and wood duck, also feed on the acorns. Caterpillars feast on the young leaves and buds and, as a result, can do so much damage that sometimes the tree dies.

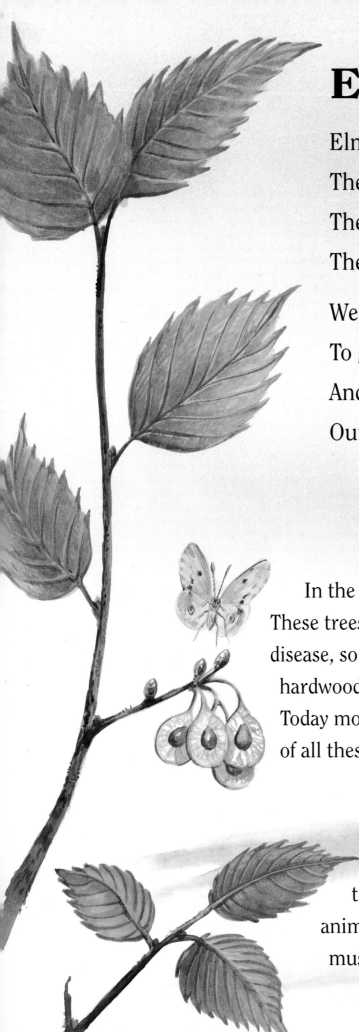

Elm

Elm trees grow mostly in the east,
Their wood is very tough;
They live for years and grow up tall,
Their bark is grey and rough.

We plant elm trees along our streets
To give us summer shade,
And out of elm, long years ago,
Our hockey sticks were made.

In the early days, hockey sticks were made out of elm These trees became scarce after they were attacked by a disease, so hockey sticks were then made from other hardwoods, such as birch, ash, hickory and maple. Today most hockey sticks are made out of a combination of all these woods, or from synthetics.

Elm is used to make barrels, boxes, piano frames, boat frames, and caskets.

The seeds and buds of this medium sized tree are food for songbirds, game birds and animals such as the deer and rabbit. Beavers and muskrats feed on the bark.

Tulip Tree

There are flowers on this poplar,

So it's called the tulip tree;

It grows across Ontario;

And some places in B.C.

This lovely tree grows tall and straight,

Its leaves are green and square;

They turn yellow when the autumn wind

Sends them dancing through the air.

Can you imagine a tree with the name of a flower?

Most trees have leaves that are rounded or pointed, but the tulip tree has leaves that are almost square. Its leaves are very distinctive and have the shape of a tulip. This is why this tree received its name.

This tall, beautiful tree also known as a yellow pine is classed as a hardwood tree. This is because it has broad leaves, rather than the kind of needles that are found on pine or fir. Its wood is soft and easy to work with. It is used to make furniture, toys, and some musical instruments.

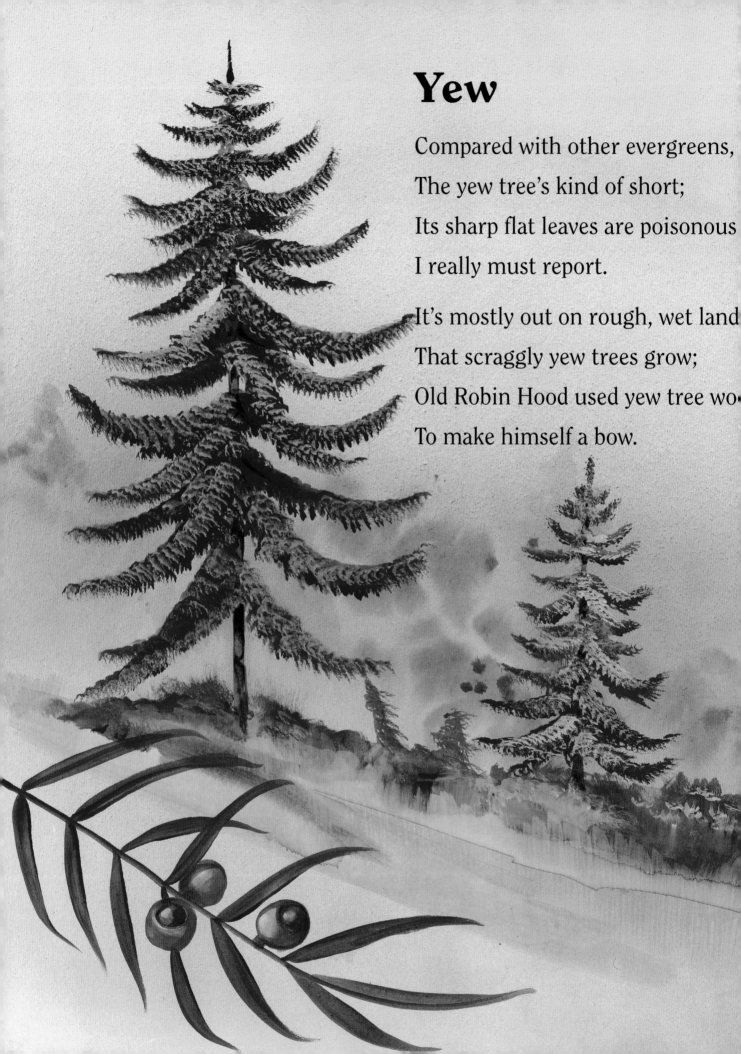

Yew

Compared with other evergreens,
The yew tree's kind of short;
Its sharp flat leaves are poisonous
I really must report.

It's mostly out on rough, wet land
That scraggly yew trees grow;
Old Robin Hood used yew tree wood
To make himself a bow.